Full Circle

Full Circle

To Cindy—
write with
courage
Elizabeth Thomas

poems by
Elizabeth Thomas

Hanover Press, Ltd.
Newtown, CT

Full Circle

Published in the United States by

Hanover Press, Ltd.
P. O. Box 596
Newtown, CT 06470-0596
www.hanover-press.com

Manufactured in the United States of America

ISBN 1-887012-16-8

*To my father
who taught me the power of words
and to my mother
who taught me how to use them.*

Full Circle

On Aging 3

Betrayal (1) 5

Never Been Kissed (2) 8

The Worm Turns (3) 10

Like a Thunderbolt 12

The Father 15

Peace Mama 17

Live at the Demo 18

Silent but Deadly 22

On Summer 24

School's Out 27

Free Fall 28

Rites of Passage 30

May 17th 33

Revelation 37

Night 39

Tight 41

For Father Cardenal 42

Almost Touching 47

Fade 49

Life Line 51

Impact 52

Sometimes You Have to Laugh 54

Tangled 56

The Sound of Your Voice 58

Skilled Nursing 59

Ebb Tide 61

Daughter

On Aging

At 3
you saved me
from the drooling mouth of the dog next door.
We later became friends
(the dog and I)
but that moment when you leapt the fence
and raced across the yard
to pull me into your protective space
is always part of me.

At 8
when we built the treehouse
and I stood on the ledge
all the way up
and you said, "Jump. I'll catch you. Trust me.",
I barely thought twice before throwing my body into the air,
into your arms.

At 13
you let me cry
then dried my tears
because the kids next door said my chest was too small
and my nose too big.
You didn't tell me not to care.
You just held me until I didn't care so much.

And when I told you at 20
how much I was in love,
you said you'd love me always.
And at 30
when I told you it was over,
you were still there to hold me.

Now I'm 41
and it's you with the drooling mouth,
you who needs protection.
I want to wipe your tears
but you push me away.

Don't tell me not to care,
it hurts too much this time.
We both know that.
Let me hold you close.

"Daddy...

    Jump."

Betrayal (1)

When I was eight
I had a pig,
a very special pig,
belly hung low
scraping the floor
with the weight of it's bounty.
My pig dined on shiny coins,
not nickels and dimes,
but silver half dollars.
Daddy so proud
as we would slip them through the slot,
one after the other.
Some nights he would come home
and awaken me to sounds of silver
dropping to my pillow.
I imagined us on deserted islands,
sea chests made of copper and wood,
my father a mighty one-eyed pirate
protecting the loot
for his lady fair.

When I was eight
you could get into the Sunday matinee for fifty cents
and a quarter would buy five pieces of candy.
A chocolate bar, wax lips, Good & Plenty, Pixie Stix, and
      a box of Goobers
to be thrown once the lights went down.
Of course,
a shiny half dollar could buy you twice that
or be shared with a convincing older brother.
My mother, happy to be rid of us,
would pay for the movie.
The rest was up to us.

I'm not pleading innocence,
but it was never my idea
(I was only eight, after all)
to lay open that pig,
scrape her hole until she bled shiny coins.

My brother always performed these illegal abortions
while I kept watch
trying to avoid the disappointment in the eyes of my pig.
We'd replace her nameless offspring
with shiny nuts and washers,
hardly an even swap,
then off we'd go
my guilt disappearing
before the first cartoon had ended.

Now, my father was no fool!
"Let's open her up!" he said one day.
And my brother,
even less a fool,
decided it was a good time to visit friends.
I begged and pleaded for the life of my pig.
"It's a special pig!" I cried.
"She's hardly fattened up!"
Still...down came the hammer.
Sharp shards of ceramic yellow
flew about the room.
I hoped one would poke my eye out
and cause distraction.
But no, there on the table
lay a few nickels and dimes,
far fewer still
silver half dollars,
and an enormous litter of nuts and washers.
My downcast eyes could count them all.
No treasure this!

When I finally looked up
he sadly shook his head,
but it was his eyes that spoke to me
of faith lost and disappointment shared.
I remember those eyes well
and throughout my life
they have always conveyed
the depth of emotion that words cannot.

My father's eyes were the very essence
of language and love.
He would never raise a hand to me,
it was not necessary.
A slap is over quickly.
His eyes haunt me always.

Never Been Kissed (2)

When I was sixteen
I had it all.
Honor student, without really trying,
debate team, ski club.
Plenty of friends,
and though not the most popular,
we were well within the boundaries of cool.

Then I met Tommy.
He was my boyfriend but he was no boy.
Twenty-one years old
with his license and a car.
He was everything a sixteen year old dreams about,
like your favorite movie star
pinned on the wall at the foot of your bed.
I'd look into his eyes
and dream about his kiss.
Only he wasn't just a photograph
or an image on the screen,
he was flesh and he liked me.
Hard to figure.
In biology class
it was a well-known fact I weighed less
than Weird Harold on the Bill Cosby Show.
I had no chest to speak of
and far less glamour.
We dated.
He said he loved me.

When I was sixteen
I sat alone in a gray clinic
staring up at yellowed posters of young women
holding the hands of drooling children.
The children always smiled,
but in the eyes of the women
there was helplessness and fear.
And when the nurse came out with her starched, white face
I knew many lives were going to change.

The hardest thing I have ever done
was tell my father.
We'd often talked of college plans and fancy weddings.
Of course, I would
marry a doctor, a lawyer, an Indian chief.
A gas station attendant?
I kept waiting for the right moment
as a doctor might with a terminal patient.
I slept a lot, ate little,
avoided him like homework.
Then one night during a rerun of Bonanza,
my father sprawled on the couch,
I said, "Daddy, I'm going to have a baby."

I sat there quietly,
my downcast eyes counting my fingers and toes.
He too was quiet,
and when I finally looked up
his eyes were distant.
I imagined him thinking of graduations
and black satin gowns,
white lace veils and giving away the bride.
A father's first dance.
He no longer looked like a mighty pirate.
At that moment he just looked old,
except for his eyes.
They held onto me
and screamed of disappointment,
screamed of pain and loss,
screamed of what would not be.
Finally
they whispered his love.

The Worm Turns (3)

When I was nineteen
the relationship was over.
He no longer spoke of loving me.
Instead, when he chose to be home,
his words were hurled
through drunken rage,
more stinging than a slap or a shove.

My decision to leave came hard
on the backend of a savage backhand.
Under one arm
I gathered up what little I felt was mine.
Under the other arm, my son.
We walked out the door
and never looked back.

Years later
I remembered one thing left behind
belonging to my son and I.
Silver half dollars...
saved over time by my father and I
(when he learned to trust me again).
Tom and I had put them aside for our son
in a wooden chest
high in a bedroom closet.
I called and the following day Tom's truck was in my driveway.
He handed me a paper bag
and left me standing by the road.

At the kitchen table
I poured out the bag
not believing my eyes.
There in front of my son and I
were a few nickels and dimes,
far fewer still
silver half dollars,
and an enormous litter of nuts and washers.
No treasure this.

I turned toward my son.
He has his father's eyes
and when he looked up at me
I wanted to shake that look
from his face,
like silver half dollars
seemingly protected in a vault of yellow.

Like a Thunderbolt

A prehistoric carnivore
all twisting arms
and impossible angles
sitting
  waiting
   wanting
some unsuspecting child
who is not paying attention
to the warning signs.
"You must stand at least this high."

"Keep your eyes open,"
my father says.
"Become part of the moment."

My hair whips my face.
My breath in short staccato.
My heart taps out an irregular back beat.
This song had better end soon
or the only thing my eyes will be watching
is lunch splatter all over my father.
Now there's a day in the park!
Ooooh noooo, we're cresting this beast.
Don't look down!
  Don't look down!

"Look down", says my father.
*"Open your eyes
and experience the ride."*

Only...
he doesn't look like my father.
His eyes
wide open
shoot flaming arrows.
His hands
which are *not* holding onto the seat bar
flail in the air like so many spider legs
and when he says, *"Open your eyes..."*

the sun catches the spittle spewing from his lips
and I can almost count the rainbowed bubbles.

And then
we're hurtling down the backend
of the biggest, boniest beast
this side of the hemisphere.
I can't breathe.
  I can't see.
    I can't talk.
I can puke though -
The skin on my face is peeling off.
My left eye has ricocheted
to the other side of my chin.
Why didn't we just go on the Merry go Round?
They're probably having fun over there.
And just when I think it's finally over
twenty-two roller-coaster cars
whip back up the tail of this nasty beast
and into a 360 degree spin.
And up and down and up and down
and down and down and...

For one quick moment
I turn to look at my father.
He's finally holding on
but his eyes tell a different story.
And the set of his mouth
tells a different story.
He's not afraid.
He's not impressed.
He's a man.
He fought in the big one.
He's lived through worse
and will tell you all about it.
No pre-historic pile of bones
is going to take him down
shake him down
or break him down.

The embrace of this moment is a gift
he passes onto me...his only daughter.
OK ... Alright... *I get it*!
I nod my head
wipe the puke from my mouth
loop my arm through his
and turn forward in my seat.
Eyes
　　wide open.

The Father

I recall
Sunday mornings as a child,
Momma waking us early
so we could visit God.
She'd scrub the sleep from my face,
wet down my hair,
smooth out my pillow head,
dress me up like a precious doll,
feathered hat and all.
Then we'd kiss my father goodbye.
Daddy never came to church with us.
I figured he must know God real well
to get off so easily,
though he always gave us a quarter for the basket.
Momma said he liked to pray alone.
Seeing as how he had five kids
she was probably onto something,
but me,
I thought God must visit him at our house
while we went to church.
Convinced, I faked sick one Sunday
but Daddy just lay there in bed,
reading the newspaper
and doing the crossword puzzle.
God never showed up
and I didn't get to play outside all afternoon.
I used to think my father was a lot like God.
When I sinned,
like the time I faked sick,
I sinned against him.
When I prayed to be forgiven
it was my father's face I saw
rising above the altar -
silent.
Words were seldom necessary.
God had nothing to do with my tears.

Going to church
was a lot like visiting my widowed aunt.

I had to sit quietly,
hands tightly folded in my lap,
scarcely breathing,
afraid of waking the ghosts
I knew were hiding in the other room.
I'd pretend to listen to adults
talk about stuff I did not understand
and if I was good
my aunt would give me a piece of candy.
The same thing happened at church,
but the candy wasn't sweet
and often stuck to the roof of my mouth.

When church was finally over
we'd stop at the bakery
for donuts and coffee to go.
Arriving home
we'd tiptoe into my father's room,
his favorite donuts hidden behind our backs.
Just once
I wanted to catch him dancing with the angels,
but instead,
there he would be
still lying in bed,
newspapers spread around him
like apostles praying at his feet.
And in those quiet moments,
even then
I think I understood.
He didn't need their faith and devotion.
He only needed us
jumping up on the bed
to give him honey-dipped kisses
and argue over who would get the funnies first.
I can still see him smiling
over the top of the newspaper
knowing he was blessed.

In the name of the Father...
Amen.

Peace Mama

Like a terrible secret,
you whispered to me
of shame, blood, and sanitary napkins.
I was only ten years old.
What did I know?
It had to be a dirty word.
So I found a spray paint can and
went down to the school yard.
All I remembered was something about a "period"
and sprayed the word DOT... D-O-T,
in bright red on the side of the building
feeling smug with the knowledge of a new swear word.

Bleaching clothes was popular when I was twelve
so I dipped a cotton swab into a capful of bleach
and wrote the word "PEACE" down the fly of my jeans.
It was meant strictly in a 60's kind of way
yet you tore those pants into dusting rags
and grounded me for a week.

And when I told Joey to "go screw"
I only wanted him to leave me alone.
Instead, I got my mouth washed out with soap.

One day my friend Kerry taught me how to say "flatus cerebellum"
and I felt so...international...since I spoke a foreign language.
I didn't know it meant "farthead" until you punished me.

And you made me go to confession
when I asked why "69" was a lucky number.

Mama...
you taught me every dirty word I know!

Live at the Demo

Nearly showtime.
You stand,
foot propped on the back of a stadium chair,
staring out past cars and track
hitting off the bottle
quenching the butterflies.
I look down at the cars parked so carefully in their places.
Such a macabre contrast to their ultimate purpose.
"What's your purpose?" I wonder.
The heat of the afternoon sun beats upon our heads and backs
causing shirts to cling.
I try not to do the same.
You lean over.
Sweat drips from your chin.
"The Ford hasn't a chance."
"What about the Nova?" I ask.
"What about the Nova?"
You swallow deeply from the bottle.

The stadium begins to fill.
People push and shove,
front and center.
They know the best seats.
They've been here before.
Already sweat pours from their bodies.
The gleaming droplets
shoot arrows from their faces.
They raise mock toasts of Styrofoam cheer
to the cars of their choice.
"All drivers report to the rear of the stadium!"
I search your face - try to smile.
You flash me a thumbs up and turn to walk away,
almost forgetting the bottle still held in your hand.
One last swallow and it's mine.
I watch as you leave me.
I scream, "Crazy fool!"
but already you're part of the roar of the engines.

I sit rigid, at the edge of my chair,
ready to swoop down and save you from this death wish of yours.
Is it the only thing you call your own?

All drivers stand listening at the rear of the stadium.
"Reading 'em their last rites," someone jokes.
I don't smile,
watch the cars instead.
Someone sprayed "Happy Father's Day" in bright red
on the side of a Chrysler.
The paint hadn't dried
before the F in Father dripped down the door panel.
The speaker blasts out names for heat #1.
Yours is not called.
The crowd begins the countdown, eager to start the show.
"3 - 2 - 1 !"
What craziness is this?
They all drive backward!
"Easier on the front end," someone explains.
I turn to watch the show below.
It is difficult to see,
smoke so thick.
There is only the smash and the thud and the roar
of cars and crowd!
The choking smell of burning rubber and burning lust,
a mid-air brew bubbling in the heat of the afternoon.

I wonder at the audience -
Their passion and anger readily exposed
in their total frenzy for destruction.
My own body quakes with each collision,
yet I'm mesmerized by all below.

As the smoke clears I watch the driver of the Ford
break off a red and white stick attached to the side of his car.
"He's out of the race," explains the man beside me.
"He didn't have a chance."
Still he's hit again and again.
Forward, reverse, smash!
The crowd explodes.

It takes a while to clear the track.
The dozers come with forks in hand.
The air doesn't clear though.
The rippled waves of heat linger,
hung low over the track,
over the twisted wrecks,
over the twisted crowd.

The speaker calls the last heat.
The smell of rubber and coolant and gasoline
steams up from the cars.
The smell of sweat and fear and desire
steams up from the crowd.
I watch as you climb in where the window used to be.
Into the Nova.
"What about the Nova?"
Every muscle in my body draws taut.
"3 - 2 - 1 !"
Did you know Mom went to church today?

I am still as you "take a good one" over and over.
Forward, reverse, smash.
Over and over.
I was there when you proudly sprayed
"Rollin' Thunder" on the side of the Nova.
You ran out of room,
wondered where to put the D, the E, and the R.
I offered a suggestion.
You didn't smile.
Now it hardly matters.
The blue, fluorescent letters are smashed beyond recognition.

The center strip bursts into flames!
The crowd goes wild!
It's their show now!
They rise to the occasion.
"Burn, baby, burn!"
The heat of the flames easily blends
with the heat of their misplaced passion.
"More! More!"

Through the smoke I search for the red and white stick
on the door of number 35.
Smash!
"Please, break your stick!"
Smash!
"Dammit! Break your stick!"
But you back up again and again.
I turn my head.
"Hey, look! His stick. He's out."
Your car is disabled.
You cannot move.
You sit there, an immobile target.
Do you remember as children when we played "crash tricycles"
in the basement of the old house?
You always won.
I wonder now how you feel,
inside 35,
with a broken stick and this mania about you.
I close my eyes.

You and the dozers appear together.
You walk over,
eyes on fire.
"So, who's the craziest guy you know?"
I slowly nod my head,
reach for your hand
and quietly, gently say,
"C'mon, I'll drive you home."

God Must Have Been Having a Really Bad Day When He Created Older Brothers (Silent but Deadly)

It's dinnertime.
Joey, who considers it his privilege
and his passion
to torment me to tragic tears,
tilts briefly to one side of his chair
and smiles.
I freeze,
fork mid-air
drips spaghetti sauce
all over the table,
and immediately suck in some air.
"One, two, three..."
Sitting at the head of the table,
my father is oblivious.
He concentrates on his food
as if it may retaliate,
seldom bringing his head up for air anyway.
Mom on the other hand
claps hand to mouth
and quickly excuses herself from the table.
I am struck by the unfairness of age!
If I got up without finishing my vegetables
I'd be grounded for a week.
"98, 99, 100...*sniff*, *sniff*
Ooooh! Not long enough."

My food has begun a meltdown
more hideous than Chernobyl
and Three Mile Island combined.
I am seeing double
and my nose has started to mutate.

Joey winks and smiles
as my father looks up
and asks me to pass the peas.
I am only ten years old,
but it becomes quite clear to me,
with men in charge of this country
no wonder it's in such a mess!

My lungs are about to explode
and I know I must breathe,
yet there is still a moistness in the air
and I am prepared to die
rather than submit to it's pungent pull!
That would serve them right!
Especially my mother!
After all, she left me out here.

But...
there's a baseball game at 6:00
and my team has a shot at the Championships.
Who would play second base?
Certainly not Joey...
although if he keeps this up
he might make an "explosive" pitcher!
Hmmm...let's see.
Death,
Baseball.
Baseball,
Death.
Hmmm...
"198, 199 ... *sniff, sniff*
Uuuuugggghhhh..."

On Summer

We crawl
under the yellow forsythia
clustered and dangling by the side of the path
that leads down to the playground.
Wriggling on stomachs and elbows
we find the hollowed out space
just big enough for two small bodies
and a picnic lunch.
Unpacking our bags
we settle down to peanut butter with no crusts
and from our thermos'
we pour icey cold milk
made magical through a straw shaped like Mickey.
As we share our desserts
we watch red sneakers race by
to wait for a turn on the merry go round
trailing laughter and sunshine and summer.

Mother

School's Out

My son weighs heavy in my arms
while stadium seats
shadow us from above.
Rays of sun try to draw us out
but darkness rocks me,
smoothes my creases.
I know I should be standing with my friends,
not here in the dark.
I should be stepping out
into the rest of my life,
not trying to take care of a new life.

The names of my classmates are announced
and I watch as they move forward.
The noise wakes my son
and he is cranky.
Wiping my nose on my sleeve
we turn to leave.
I hear the sound of "Long and Winding Road"
by the Beatles
crackle over the speakers.

Free Fall

People smile and tell me I'm the lucky one
and we've just begun
think I'm gonna have a son.

"They" are pregnant
and already he is the doting father.
Helping her into a chair,
bringing a glass of water,
patting her on the head as if *she* were the child.
I look into her eyes.
She is all confidence and ease.
When pregnant with my own son
I worried always and questioned and cried.
At 17, I was dropped off at the hospital door
alone and afraid.
The cord connecting me to my family severed
9 months earlier.

I want to feel her belly.
Feel the life growing there.
Wrap my arms around it
and whisper,
"Everything'll be all right."
I want to feel the kick and the turn,
add a little english,
experience the spin.
It's like ... free falling
and you, Mother,
are the net.
Again I look into her eyes
wondering if she realizes the extent of her passion,
the commitment she embraces.
I know the pain of child-rearing
can sometimes be
many times worse than the pain of childbirth.

Thinking of my own son
I tally up the blessings
and the where-did-I-go-wrongs
trying to balance the scale,

knowing it tips more to one side
as he gets older,
realizing I no longer have all the answers
and sometimes don't even understand the questions.
It's been a long time
since I have wrapped my arms around him
and whispered,
"Everything'll be all right."

I place my hands on my own belly
knowing it is empty
and can no longer provide.
He is all I have.
If I could go back 20 years
would I do it again?
"People smile and tell me I'm the lucky one."
Would I do it again?
"And we've just begun."
Through him I give and gain balance.
A necessary grounding,
our roots gently tangled up
in family and commitment.
This sometimes brings pain
but it also carries with it spirit and life.
Would I do it again?

"Think I'm gonna have a son."

Rites of Passage

I remember the first time,
excitement causing my hands to tremble.
I carefully reached down
just above my ankle
and brought the razor up
over the tickle of hair on my leg
slowly past my knee and onward
to the very top of my thigh.
I   was a woman!
Isn't it funny how now shaving my legs
is an incredible pain in the ass
and I wish I had listened to my mother when she said,
 "Don't shave your legs!"

Or the first time,
legs slightly parted,
not quite sure how to put it on.
I considered advice from friends who knew
and a brief, dark discussion with my mother,
then I fumbled with the hooks
(no beltless pads back then)
and tucked the whole wad into my panties.
I stood straight and tall.
A couple more adjustments
and I knew I had a friend.
Of course, now my friend
is just my *"friend"*
and unless it's late,
it's just another pain in the ass.

And remember when you thought they'd never grow?
I'd stand in the privacy of the bathroom
(the only door with a lock)
and pull and plead to God,
"Make them grow!
Please, make them big!"
I had four brothers.
The odds were against me.
Finally, the day came and my mother brought me
to Sage Allen's department store.

While she waited outside the dressing room
I took off my tee shirt,
strapped myself in,
and started my engines.
I ... am ... WOMAN !
Hear me roar!

Then there was makeup.
I still see myself in the mirror
applying eyeliner, eye shadow,
mascara so thick I could hardly blink,
and ruby red lipstick.
I was only twelve,
but at that moment I knew I could pass for twenty-one.
My lipstick alone spoke years of experience
and besides...
I wore a bra.

And who could forget
the first time they went *"all the way"*?
I always imagined it would be at the beach
with the sun and the sand,
the waves rolling in,
sweat glistening upon our naked bodies,
gently caressing, madly in love,
we would reach a fever pitch,
it would be like a million fourth of Julys,
together...
never ending.

As I remember
it happened on graduation night.
We were headed for the beach
but wound up in the basement
of my boyfriend's parent's house,
on an old musty couch.
I remember springs in my back,
beer on his breath
and the sound of his parent's television set
never ending.

Here I am ten years
and three children later.
Though I can look back
upon those initiations into womanhood
and smile at the awkwardness
and absurdity of it all,
I know my oldest daughter is just steps away
from that first, terrifying plunge
and all I want to say to her is,
"Honey, whatever you do -

>   *Don't shave your legs!"*

May 17th

Ten feet from the open door of the Dairy Bar
I am greeted by smells of summer.
Hot dogs twirling on a grill
french fries and melted cheese
the comforting scent of chocolate sauce.
Standing in a line that spirals out the door
like the top of a soft serve cone
I close my eyes.
Once again I am a young girl
in the back seat of my parent's station wagon
cresting the road that leads to the beach.
Summer seemingly endless
like the sea laid out before me
a sparkling magician's cape.

As I order a vanilla chocolate twist
a group of young boys, just off a baseball win
walk up in grass-stained T-shirts
and hard hats they are reluctant to remove.
They jostle to be first in line
loudly remind each other
of a fly ball caught in the tip of a glove
a double play
a homerun hit in the bottom of the sixth
punctuating each statement with a punch or push.
These small wins
large in their minds:
heroes, masters of their world, kings for a day.
This moment, so vivid
as colorful as the jars of sprinkles
which line the shelves
just beyond their reach.

And as someone's mother pays for their cones
I watch as they lick quickly
the ice cream already beginning to melt.

Teacher

Revelation

His T-shirt says, "I am God".
I think
"Well, my lucky day!"
I'll run up
shake his hand
ask for an autograph.
I might never have this chance again.
But, as God sits there
waiting to step into the Vice Principal's office
I look closely at the faded T-shirt
two sizes too big
sneakers older than he is
thin legs swinging
barely long enough to reach the floor
dirty hands massaging a dirty forehead and think
"This is not God."
This is a little boy
who maybe swore in the lavatory
or tussled on the playground.
A child who probably forgot to eat breakfast
did not expect a good-bye kiss.
When he gets home from school today
he'll let himself in with the key
that hangs around his neck.
He might help himself to Twinkies and a glass of Coke
a microwaved pizza in front of the TV.
He struggles to raise his head.
The circles under his eyes slope toward his chin
pick up the lines around his mouth
and carry them down as well.
It's not easy taking care of the world.

Using the back of his hand
he trails snot and tears across his face
into his hair
which heads out in all directions
as if just lifted from a pillow.
He looks neglected
like homework over a long weekend.
This boy ain't been loved in a long time.

I want to walk over
kneel on both knees
use my sleeve to clean his cheeks
kiss his feet
tie his sneakers.
He looks up
and in his eyes I see my own son.
Unable to look away
I want to say something
make some excuse
beg for forgiveness.
But this is God.
What could I possibly say
he does not already know?

Night

I watch the students file into the room.
My eyes follow a tall boy
dressed entirely in black.
Except for his face and two middle fingers
which poke through black fishnet sleeves
he could be night.
Black leather vest
black shirt underneath
black torn jeans
long straight black hair
black hat worn low over his eyes.
He makes his way to the last row
black boots scraping the floor
as if weighted with rock.
He squeezes himself into a seat
not designed for his large frame.
It takes him several minutes to finally sit still
and then for the next 20 minutes
he does not move.
As I stand at the front of the room
talking about the creative process
his head remains bowed
and he becomes one with his desk.
When asked to take out paper and pen
he finally stirs
reaches into a worn black leather bag
and pulls out the stub of a pencil
and to my surprise
what looks to be a writing journal.
I ask the class to write "Who am I"
at the top of the page
then describe their essence as something in nature.
I look at him and again think "night".
He writes
head close to the paper.
Black hair like seaweed
tangles in his words.
His long arms surround the notebook
as if to protect it from harm.
A caress.

When the buzzer blares the end of class
he takes his time collecting himself
and when everyone has left
walks slowly toward me.
He hands me his writing
torn from the journal
and asks if I'll read it.
It takes everything I know about being a teacher
not to jump up and down
throw my arms around him
and shout, "Yes! Yes! Of course I'll read it!"
He buries his hands into the pockets of his jeans
while I read a poem about a friend who's gone away
and how he'd like Spring to return
give birth to their friendship again.

His vest opens as his boots dig the floor
and I can see the writing on his shirt.
It says, "Misfit".
Here in this room though
we both know
         he belongs.

Tight

Alone at the back of the room
she tries to become one
with the lines of her chair.
Hard lines drawn
not just because her name is Jennifer
and the rest of the class are called
Raul, Jose, Yuly, Rashonda.

No,
she is fat.
Elbows and chin dimple like dough.
The seams of her jeans
stretch across her thighs
like the smile pulling her face.
And she is so painfully accountable
that from the front of the room
where I talk about the writing process
even I feel the edge of the razor.
She tries to ignore its sharpness
cutting deep
leaving the tough skin of scar and
"Okay...I know I'm fat...but I am so hungry."
She is a stone
motionless, unflinching.

When I ask the class
what "tools" are most important
to help us through life?
"Brains"
"Money"
"Strength"
it's as if someone reached over and wound her up.
She lifts her head
opens her mouth
and with a sweep of her hands she says
"Friendship."
The rest of the class roll their eyes
and laugh among themselves.

For Father Cardenal

She's a foot tapping
pen clicking
hair flipping
eyebrow raising
head rocking
teeth sucking
"who the fuck are you?"
kind of 90's
kind of girl

and she can't help but giggle
at the man who reads poetry
in front of the room because
"poetry is stupid."
He is unfazed
so intent on his words
and the history they convey.
In broken English and in fierce Spanish
he wants them to understand
the conviction of liberation
and how in a true revolution
nine year olds may lead armies
die for a righteous cause.
Mockingly she turns toward her neighbor
rolls her eyes and fakes a yawn.
From both sides she is shushed.
"Why should I listen to him?"

Rocking in her chair
she mouths the words to a song
hands never still, tapping the backbeat.
Like a point of light in the dark
my own eyes track her
and I blink at the flame.
She just can't sit still
and finally the teacher
with Mrs. Potato Head lips
leans back and glares in her direction.
Like the poet himself
she is unfazed.

He recites a poem about the beating of wings
against the bars of cages
and how when he finally returned
to the mountains of his native Nicaragua
so many young people were dead or disappeared.
"During this revolution
it was a crime to be young,"
he tells the audience of high school students.
When he came home he kissed the ground
knowing it was sacred
a "great tomb of martyrs".
"How can anyone just sit here and listen to this guy?
What is he talking about?"
Except for his black beret
he looks like Santa Claus.
"Where's my present?"

In a choked voice
the last poem is about a poet...his nephew
who shouts, "Free homeland or death"
and accomplishes both by the age of 20.
The word "death" has caught her roving attention.
"There ain't nothin' I would give my life for!
Get this guy out of here!"

He's a worn down
sandal wearing
gotta say it
"Can you hear me?"
inside out
out of time
kind of 90's
kind of poet.

"You can't teach me nothing!
Go ahead...I dare you!"

Daughter

Almost Touching

My blanket is fraying
      the edges wearing thin from
            too many spin cycles.

It used to be bright paisley pink
with flying bears
      reaching for the stars
            And lots of pots
                  of dreams.

The makers of Tide
            lied
              about being color safe.

My blanket is fraying
the satin worn
with time and aging.

When I was a little girl
I never sucked my thumb
but sometimes on laundry day
I'd wait in the crawl space
beneath the stairs
and suck the skin
           right here
between thumb and finger.

Joey sucked his thumb
till he was 14 years old.
Mom would rub garlic all over it
before he'd go to bed at night.
She thought garlic would cure anything
including my pinworms
which she said I got
from eating raw spaghetti.
She'd string cloves of garlic into a necklace
slipping it over my head
while I was sleeping.
      I almost strangled twice.

But the pinworms ate well
and Joey's orthodontist
had two Porsches and a beach house.

My blanket is fraying.
Falling apart all around me.
There was once a time
I could wrap myself up

                and disappear,
but it's fading away.

I now see through
      the flying bears

         through the promise
                of the dreams

And I'm floating past the stars

            into black...

Fade

I stand quietly
and watch her from the open doorway.
She sits alone at the kitchen table,
hair pulled back
into curlers and bobby pins.
The fishnet bonnet I have known all of my life
still holds her into place.
One hand holds a cup of coffee
while the other hand taps out a beat
on the scratched Formica tabletop.
What song can she be thinking of, I wonder?
It has been many years since music has played in this house.
As I watch
her eyes close
and her head begins to sway from side to side.
A slight smile,
a deep breath,
and she pushes herself away from the chair,
wraps her arms around her narrow body
and begins to weave across the kitchen floor.
I am stunned
as I watch her dance
to this music I cannot hear.
Suddenly, I am transported with her.
We glide together on sandy beaches,
water kisses our ankles and feet.
Handsome men stand in line.
She is young and beautiful
and they push their way to her.
She smiles and flirts
and plays the game well.

I have never known her this way.
To me she has always just been "Mother".
An adult woman in my life
who I have loved in a distant,
hands-off kind of way.
She has always taken care of me

and as an adult now myself,
I do my best to take care of her.

What must she have been like as a young girl?
A tomboy I'm told,
all tough and tender.
More apt to whistle through her fingers
than whisper softly in your ear.
When she was young
her hair was worn loose,
wild, black curls of abandon and youth.
What did she expect out of life back then?
As I watch her dance around this cluttered kitchen,
hair pulled tightly into that fishnet bonnet,
I imagine she expected
more than this.

I stand
watching her turn,
watching this kaleidoscope of motion
who is my mother,
is my blood
and I am sad
I never knew her this way.

Then she sees me standing there
and stops in mid-sweep.
She looks into my eyes,
sees the tears,
slowly shakes her head
and whispers, "No, no."
and smiles.
Then this woman,
my mother,
reaches out,
takes me into her arms,
and together we dance
into a dazzling sunset.

Life Line

When the phone rang
I knew
before any words were spoken.
I could see each syllable floating
like a helium balloon
rising dangerously close to electrical wires.
I knew, as daughters know,
feeling her uncertainty and pain,
feeling it reach out to me
and take hold.
All I could do was gently cradle it,
allow her the quietude of my womb,
take care of her for awhile.

Now in dim hospital hallways
I stand helpless
as she is taken from me.
I want to reach out and hold her
but she has never been comfortable
with physical displays of affection,
so I hold back
my arms and my tears,
kiss her briefly on the head
as she is wheeled away into the arms of strangers.

I linger as they move away
still gently tethered to the umbilical cord,
feel the tug as she disappears around a corner,
the connection,
the pain
sharp and poignant as childbirth.
I am connected to her.
The cord extends back to her mother
who is connected to her own mother
and on and on through time.
It reaches through generations of strong and capable women,
each linking arms to surround her and protect her
and I -
I find comfort in their power.

Impact

I'm falling
and instead of waking up
my body smashes to earth
into a million fragile pieces.
The sound of impact
throws back my head
and I open my eyes.
She is still there.
Her heart still beats.
The jagged red line
tells me so.
The beep, beep, beep
tells me so.
She is uncharacteristically quiet.
Breathe, I whisper, breathe.
As I watch her ancient chest
through the thin white johnny,
I do not see it rise and fall.
I am thankful for the beeping.

I have been sitting in this same chair forever.
My eyes trace the lines of her face,
deep canyons
well traveled and lived in.
Last week she stood at this window,
intravenous pole standing tall
like a faithful dog on her right
while she pointed down at gray concrete and blacktop.
She grew up in this city,
was a child in this city,
and like a magician
she waved her hand and brought it all to life for me -
pointing out streets where she grew up,
now office buildings and carry outs.
She knew exactly where her home once stood.
I too remember it vaguely from my childhood.
Sunday dinners with my Nonie,
playing games with my cousins.

Again, she waved her hand
and this time she *too* came alive -
a little girl skipping down the sidewalk
introducing me to the hot dog man,
the shoemaker,
my grandfather.
I felt large and clumsy
as I tried to keep up.
She pointed to a parking lot
where she played baseball with my uncles.
I saw her there with skinny legs
and a powerful arm from third base.
Thanks to her,
I too can make the throw.
She pointed out a corner
and I watched her fall in love with my father
selling newspapers the first time she saw him
and my eyes stung
with the pain of unseemly aging.
I've heard the story many times before
but that day, at this window,
I too was there.

We stood together
looking out at this city
and I watched her grow up,
watched her live.
And now,
as I fall back to earth
feeling the impact of her life
I scream out,
"This is not fair!"
And the only response I get is
"Beep, beep, beep."

Sometimes You Just Have to Laugh

It's time.
Mom has come to visit
and may not go home.
The doctors peeled back
half her skull,
massaged her brain
until it is difficult to remember who I am
or even who she is.
Until each word is an effort
and much of what she has always taken for granted,
like tying her shoes,
must be considered fully,
each step of the process broken down.
"The shoe goes on your foot, Ma."
Her frustration is as tangible
as my emotions.

So we look for humor to balance the pain.
Like when the tin foil began to disappear
and I watched her use it to dry the clean dishes
which she then put in the dishwasher
just in case.
This Italian woman who at meals
always served herself last
now takes her food first
and the rest of us are on our own.
I smile and think, "All right, Ma!"
The helpful part of her personality
seems not to have been damaged
so I explain for the fifth time
how to run the washing machine
knowing my white panties will never be white again.
I'm getting used to the subtle shades of greens and blues.

While still at the hospital she watched with glee and superiority
as the man beside her ate his pudding with a butter knife
as she cut her meatloaf with a soup spoon.
When asked what the hospital served for dinner the night before,
she happily replied *"peanut butter and hash."*

"Was it good?"
"I could have made better," she said.

This woman,
once as comfortable in the kitchen
as most of us are sleeping,
uses a gravy ladle to stir her coffee
and insists on keeping the sugar in the microwave.

"Hey, Ma. How about when we used to play Hit the Bat
at the old house?
You sure had a good arm!"
And she looks at me through foggy eyes
and wonders who that woman was.

My son just turned 21 and I find myself again
taking care of a child.
I have to laugh at God's sense of humor,
and it is this laughter
which guides me through each day.
At night when I tuck her in
and the tears threaten to finally come,
instead of crying
I kiss her goodnight and say,
 "Hey, Ma, did you brush your teeth yet?"
"Whose teeth?"
"I love you."

Tangled

I see his head
over the top of the chair.
He is a big man
even when hunched over his crossword puzzle.
Morning coffee steams beside him
and he does not notice me staring.
At seventy-five years old
few streaks of white mark his hair.
And though he does not believe
in touching it up,
he is not against combing it up and over
front and center,
to give him some bangs
and that wind-blown look.
Lately when I come to visit
he seems a stranger to me,
someone I have known
but cannot put a name to.
This consideration is often exciting
as I change our past,
play with possibilities.

You see,
he is an Italian father
in every sense of the word
and I am his only daughter.
I've spent much of my life
trying to measure up
to his expectations of who I should be.
With three brothers before me and one long after,
I was angel dust from Heaven
sprinkled into his life,
floating in a ray of sunlight
streaming through the windowpane.
He would buy me tea sets
and dresses fit for a princess,
treat me like the dolls
he insisted I play with.

What I wanted was a truck
and PF Flyers -
hamsters and a baseball.
I got the twelve-key plastic organ
while my brothers got the drums.
Still it hurt me more to disappoint him
than it did to acquiesce,
so I would tie the ribbons in my hair
and once again around my heart.

He did not hold me back intentionally.
He was just too limited to ever question decisions made
or examine a failure to communicate.
When I chose to step over the lines
he drew around me,
I did so in a big way.
Completely off the page.

Yet now,
it is me he looks to for company and conversation.
I sometimes see shadows in the corner
and find it difficult to adjust to this man,
this stranger.
As our roles reverse
my expectations are not as high as his were.
When he repeats a story I have heard many times before,
I smile and listen again.
And when he falls asleep
I tuck him in and kiss his cheek
as he once did mine.
I think perhaps if I could change the past,
he'd love me less
and himself more.
Instead of trying to build my life,
he'd have finished building his own.
Then maybe
the ribbons would not be tied so tightly,
the knots easier to untangle.

The Sound of Your Voice

I sit in a chair by the side of your bed
hold your good hand
talk to you about everything
including the weather.
Your eyes are closed
but I know you are listening.
When asked a question
you squeeze once for "yes"
twice for "no".
I try to remember the sound of your voice
calling me in from play
helping me with homework
talking on the phone
asking why I haven't been by.
The last time I heard you speak
we talked over ice cream sundaes with extra hot fudge.
You told me stories of Nonie and Grandpapa
of Italy and coming home, Papa, coming home.
So enchanted was I by these stories not heard before.
Not like when you ate three double splits on a dare.
You were passing on history
too precious to be silenced by a stroke.
The next morning we got the call.
Papa, I do not want to talk to doctors anymore.
Tell me what to do.

When I was a little girl
the sound of your voice
could raise the hair on my arms
but growing up
it was seldom directed at me in anger.
There are not enough numbers
to count how many times you said
      "I love you."
And now I would promise anything
to hear you speak those words once more.
Instead, you squeeze my hand
three times...
and I lay my head down on the bed
falling asleep
to the sound
of your breathing.

Skilled Nursing

I walk the dim hallway.
Mary in F2 calls out from her wheelchair,
"Is everything all right, Honey?"
As always I answer,
"Yes, fine. Thank you."
But in this place
we both know I am lying.
Each doorway frames the same picture.
Wheels instead of legs.
Blank stares at silent televisions.
Endless days,
sepia-tone
corners torn.
"Is everything all right?"

In F7
a woman lies
splayed across her bed
like the damaged petals of a crushed flower.
Her johnny has opened
as she struggles in her sleep.
I quietly step into the room,
tug gently at the cotton,
cover her wrinkled breasts
which hang like weighted stockings.

Further down the hallway
a child's high-pitched giggle
sounds so irreverent,
but I smile at its self-importance
and think how the memories of today
will carry someone through the week.
Still smiling
I step around Charlie.
It is rumored he does not have a room
since he is always in the hallway.
He sits hunched over in his chair,
head in both hands.

Lightly, I touch his shoulder
to ask if he is staying out of trouble.
He looks up angry
as if someone switched the station
during his favorite show.
When he sees me though, he smiles.

He watches
as I step into my father's room.
Papa sits on his own four wheels
staring intently out the window.
He is so thankful for that window
and I am struck
as I have been many times
at how age reconstructs
our image of wealth and worth,
our measurement of good fortune.
When my father hears me enter
he turns,
shifts his line of vision
until he is focused on my face.
I pause,
give him time to process,
wait for his smile.
It takes so little to make him a rich man.

His roommate Walter has a visitor today.
He sits with his own daughter
and they quietly talk.
I hear her say,
"Dad, what would you like me to bring you
        next time I come visit?"
"Nothing."
"Oh, come on. You must want something."
The room is still for many minutes.
As I sit holding my father's hand
Walter finally says,
"A peach...
I'd like a nice, ripe peach."

Ebb Tide

She stands in the doorway waving
half in, half out.
Sharp edge of the frame cuts her in two.
We said our good-byes hours ago
but she,
unwilling to let me leave,
creates a current with her movements,
tugs me back to the kitchen table
coffee cup in hand
to talk about native strawberries
and what she will cook for dinner.
We do not journey far
and always come back to where we began.

I balance a bag of tomatoes she has given me,
struggle with car keys.
Like a buoy tied to something deeper,
she watches from the door and waves.
When I again look up
she moves toward me
   stroke, breath
    stroke, breath
away from this house
where they have lived since before I was born.
   stroke, breath
In the parlor he silently sits.
Tints of blue and gray flicker on his lopsided face.
Only his eyes move now.
   stroke,
    breath

Dishes are done.
Laundry sways in the breeze.
Days and nights stretch beyond the horizon.
Hypnotic,
   stroke, breath
Arctic,
   stroke, breath
Surge,
   stroke
Recede.

A Note From the Author

In March 1996, my mother had emergency surgery for two left-side brain aneurysms. Three days later my father had a massive stroke. Since the days of walking back and forth between their hospital rooms, our lives have changed completely. Through the tears, and yes...through the laughter, we have reacquainted ourselves with each other in ways never anticipated and have loved each other in ways not expected.

Many of the poems in this book were written from these experiences. For those readers who find themselves saying, "I understand...", this collection of poetry is offered as a celebration of you. The book is also for my husband for being there through it all and putting up with me. And it is for my children Kevin, Kristen, Emmy and Jeremy. "You better love me...this much."

About The Author

ELIZABETH THOMAS has always believed in the
concept of "poetry as remedy" and throughout her life
uses writing as a tool to help her understand things
that don't make sense. As a daughter, mother and
teacher this awareness has provided joy and solace,
laughter and tears, but most of all...a personal
journey that continues to astonish her.

Elizabeth is the Program Director for Words Alive, a
greater Hartford, CT in-school writing program. She is
also a member of Words in Motion, the Windham Area
Poetry Project and Poetry Live in Litchfield, CT – all are
in-school writing programs. She is the Webmaster for
a teen writing e-zine and an organizer/coach for the
National High School Poetry Slam. She provides writing
programs for schools and organizations through work-
shops/presentations that promote literacy and the power
of both the written and spoken word. As a poet and
performer, she is featured throughout the U.S.

She lives in CT with her husband, David, and Buca,
the dog.

Acknowledgements

"May 17th" and "Ebb Tide" first appeared in *The Underwood Review* (Hanover Press, Ltd. - November 1999)

"For Father Cardenal" first appeared in *Will Work For Peace* (1999)

"Fade" first appeared in *Articulation* (Ambergris Publishing - August 1997)

"Summer" first appeared in *The Natural Networker* (1998)